PRIMARY PARTNERS

More A-Z Activities to Make Learning Fun

for Nursery and Age 3 - Volume 2
(SUNBEAM NURSERY)

Fun-to-Make Visuals ◘ Copy-and-Create Crafts

Simple Supplies Needed ◘ Matching Thought Treats

SUPPLEMENTAL MATERIAL FOR PRIMARY LESSONS

AND FAMILY HOME EVENING USE

to Reinforce Gospel Topics

You'll Find: A-Z Topics to Match Primary Lessons

Adam   Animals   Birds & Insects   Body   Brothers & Sisters

Child   Church   Day & Night   Ears   Easter   Example

Eyes   Family   Feelings   Fish & Water Animals

Food & Clothing   Forgive   Friends   Hands   Helping   Holy Ghost

Home   Honesty   Jesus Was Born   Jesus   Love   Music

Obedience   Plan   Prayer   Prophet   Reverence   Sabbath Day

Sacrament   Scriptures   Smell & Taste   Sorry   Things

Trees, Plants & Flowers   Water

Covenant Communications, Inc.
American Fork, Utah

Printed in the United States of America
First Printing: October 1997

04 03 02 01 00 99 98 97   10 9 8 7 6 5 4 3 2 1

Primary Partners: Nursery and Age 3 Vol. 2

Covenant Communications, Inc.
ISBN 1-57734-185-6

INTRODUCTION

PRIMARY PARTNERS:
Nursery and Age 3 Vol. 2
(NURSERY & SUNBEAMS)

More A-Z Activities to Make Learning Fun

You've seen our first volume of Nursery and Age 3. Here are 46 more lesson match activities for tiny tots. The first volume activities are previewed on pages 80-84. With two activity books to choose from, you can double your fun.

Children and parents alike will love the easy, fun-to-create visuals contained in this volume. Patterns for each of the projects are actual size, ready to Copy-n-Create in minutes.

You'll enjoy using *Primary Partners* crafts and activities to supplement your Primary 1* lessons, enhance your family home evenings, and help children learn gospel principles in fun, creative ways.

HOW TO USE THIS BOOK

1. **Use the Lesson #1-46 Table of Contents** to match your lessons.

2. **Preview A-Z Table of Contents** to find pictures and subjects.

3. **Shop Ahead for Simple Supplies.** Most activities require copies of patterns, scissors, glue, tape, and crayons. Some activities require the following: string or yarn, paper punch, straws, paper cups, paper plates, zip-close plastic sandwich bags, wooden craft sticks, metal brads, seeds and dirt, popcorn or rice, and gold stars.

4. **Copy Patterns Ahead.** Most activities require cardstock paper. If this is not available, glue another piece of paper behind the copy of the activity before cutting out.

5. **Organize Activities** in a #1-46 or A-Z file ready to use. Copy instructions to include with the pattern copies and supplies.

6. **Serve Treats that Match Lesson** to enhance both learning and fun.

7. **Send Home a Show-and-Tell Sack.** The first week, decorate a sack that each child can take home to display creations.
TO MAKE SACK: (1) Copy patterns on the following page. (2) Glue Sunny Sunday Sack (top sun piece) on sack at the top of sack.
(3) Glue bottom sun piece below, gluing only 1/4" on sides and bottom only (leaving top open to create a pocket). (4) Glue stickers on sack.
(5) Fill in child's name on Parent's Note and sign your name at the bottom. Attach note to sack as child leaves, or hand note to parent.

*Primary 1 manual is published by The Church of Jesus Christ of Latter-day Saints, Salt Lake City, Utah.

Dear Parents:
This is:

_____'s
**Sunny
SUNDAY Sack**.
Each week,
please help your
child display Primary
or family home
evening creations.
    Self-esteem
builds as items are
shown and lessons
retold.
    Place creations in
the show-and-tell
pocket during the
week to reinforce the
gospel topic. Then,
when next week's
creation appears,
store past project in
the sack.

Thank you.

_____
Primary Teacher

TABLE OF CONTENTS

PRIMARY PARTNERS Nursery and Age 3 - Vol. 2   Lesson Match Activities for Primary 1 manual*

* Primary 1 manual is published by The Church of Jesus Christ of Latter-day Saints, Salt Lake City, Utah.

ADAM & Eve and Other Creations (Days 1-6 creation wristband) . . . . @

ANIMALS: I Am Thankful for Animals (favorite animal sticker fun) . . . 17, 19-20

ANIMALS: I Can Be Kind (Adam Names the Animals slide show) . . . 58-59

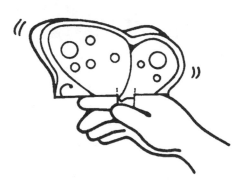

BIRDS & INSECTS: I'm Thankful For (butterfly home and finger puppet) 21-22

BODY: I Can Be Strong (Daniel Eats Good Food mouth pocket) . . . 24, 26-27

BODY: I Look Like Heavenly Father and Jesus (First Vision pop-up) . . . 1, 3

BROTHERS & SISTERS: Helping (Baby Moses in Bulrushes) 38, 40

CHILD OF GOD: (crown for a heavenly prince or princess) 1-2

CHURCH: I Can Do Many Things (church charm bracelet) 67, 71

DAY & NIGHT: Jesus Created Day & Night (day & night bracelet) 10, 12

EARS: I Am Thankful I Can Hear (listen carefully rattle) 28, 30

EASTER: Jesus Loves Me (resurrection book) 76-77

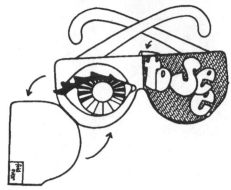

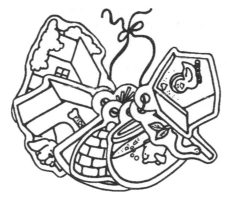

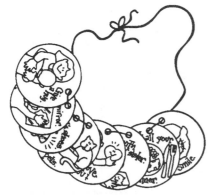

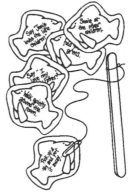

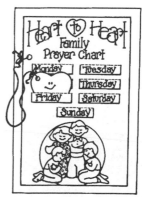

Lesson #1 *	**CHILD:** I Am a Child of God *(crown for heavenly prince or princess)*

YOU'LL NEED: Copy of crown (page 2) on cardstock paper for each child, scissors, glue or tape, and crayons

ACTIVITY: Create a crown for each child to show they are princes or princesses in Heavenly Father's kingdom.

Review the Enrichment Activity #3 (page 3) in the Primary 1 manual.*

(1) Personalize crown by drawing child's hair and clothes. (2) Color and cut out crown. (3) Glue or tape together.

TO ROLE PLAY: Lead children reverently around the room singing "I Am a Child of God," page 2 in *Children's Songbook*.

STORY OPTION: Use Baby Moses in the Bulrushes visuals on pages 39, 40 in this book to tell the story (page 2) in Primary 1 manual.*

THOUGHT TREAT: <u>Prince or Princess Cookie</u>. Roll out and cut out sugar cookie or gingerbread cookie dough. Cut out girl and boy shapes. Cut out a small crown and place on top. Frost cookies and place small candies on crown to look like jewels.

Lesson #2 *	**BODY:** My Body Looks Like Heavenly Father and Jesus *(First Vision—Jesus and Heavenly Father pop-up scene)*

YOU'LL NEED: Copy of cup label and Jesus and Heavenly Father figures (page 3) on cardstock paper, a straw and paper cup for each child, scissors, glue, tape, and crayons

ACTIVITY: Create a First Vision scene with Jesus and Heavenly Father to pop out of a paper cup to show that Joseph

Review Additional Activities #1, 2, and 3 (pages 5-6) in the Primary 1 manual.*

Smith did see that we have a body like Jesus and Heavenly Father.
1. Color and cut out cup label and Jesus and Heavenly Father images.
2. Glue and tape (to reinforce) cup label on paper cup.
3. Tape Jesus and Heavenly Father images on top of a straw.
4. Tape bottom of cup to reinforce cup to prevent tearing. Then pierce a hole in bottom of cup to insert straw.
5. Children can push and pull to make the Heavenly Father and Jesus images pop up as they remember how Joseph Smith prayed in the Sacred Grove and saw the Father and the Son.

THOUGHT TREAT: <u>"I'm Thankful for My Body" Prayer Pudding</u>. Serve children pudding from a small container. As children eat pudding, talk about things they can thank Heavenly Father and Jesus for when they pray. Say,
"I am thankful for my body, it is so neat.
I'm thankful for my eyes, nose, mouth, ears, hands, legs and feet.
I'm thankful for the gospel of Jesus Christ. It is so sweet!"

A

Glue to B

I am a ROYAL child

Glue to A

B

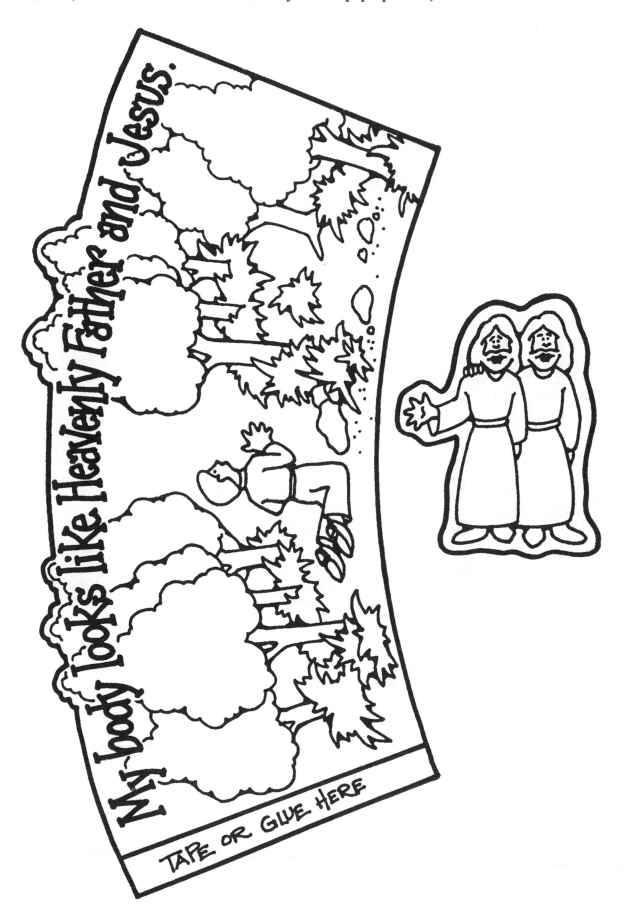

My body looks like Heavenly Father and Jesus.

TAPE OR GLUE HERE

Lesson #3*

PLAN: Heavenly Father's Plan—I Am a Child of God
(make-a-face fun)

YOU'LL NEED: Copy of face and face parts (page 5) on cardstock paper for each child, scissors, glue, and crayons

ACTIVITY: Tell children that it is Heavenly Father's plan for us to come to earth to gain a physical body that looks like him. Our body helps us to see, hear, eat, speak, and smell.

1. Cut out face parts and glue them on the face.
2. Draw and color in hair and clothing to match child.

> *Review the Enrichment Activity #1 (page 8) in the Primary 1 manual*.*

3. Children can take turns showing their picture to the class. Ask child to say something good about him/herself, e.g.: "I am pretty." "I am handsome." "I am smart." "I am happy." "I am a child of God." "I like to help." "I am nice." "I am quiet in Heavenly Father's house."

THOUGHT TREAT: <u>Funny Face Sandwich</u>. Create a sandwich filled with cream cheese, chopped boiled eggs and mayonnaise, bologna, or peanut butter and jam. Decorate sandwich with a funny face with frosting or colored cream cheese (add food coloring). Decorate sandwiches with children there, placing eyes on each sandwich first, then adding the nose, ears, and mouth.

Lesson #4*

PRAY: I Can Say "Thanks" to Heavenly Father
(many thanks mini book)

YOU'LL NEED: Copy of mini book pages (page 6) on cardstock paper for each child, scissors, stapler, and crayons

ACTIVITY: Create a miniature book with pages that show what they are thankful for.

> *Review Enrichment Activity #6 on pages 12 in Primary 1 manual*.*

1. Color and cut out book pages.
2. Staple pages together with "I thank Heavenly Father for ..." cover on top.
3. Ask them to say, "I thank thee for ..." as they name their blessings. Ask children to look at their book before they pray to remind them to thank Heavenly Father for their many blessings.
4. Teach children how to pray and say, "I thank thee for _____," as they name a blessing from the book.

THOUGHT TREAT: <u>Happy Face Finger Foods</u>. Draw a smile on a piece of paper for each child to use to hold finger foods (yummy snacks they can eat with their fingers.) Tell children to thank Heavenly Father for the food that we are so happy to eat. Finger Food Ideas: Peanut Butter sandwiches (whole sandwich cut in fourths with a frosted smile on each, bologna or cheese with smile face cut out.

PATTERN: *PLAN (I am a child of God fun face)*

I am a child of God.

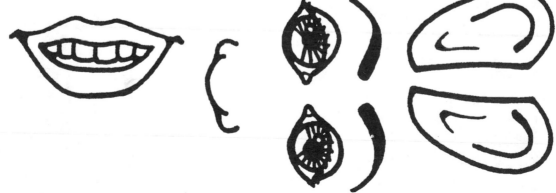

Lesson #5*	JESUS Is Heavenly Father's Son *(baby Jesus in a cradle)*

YOU'LL NEED: Copy of baby Jesus and manger (page 8) on cardstock paper for each child, scissors, glue, and crayons.

ACTIVITY: Send children home with the baby Jesus in a cradle with a note

Review Additional Activity #1 (page 14) in the Primary 1 manual.*

attached that reads: "Jesus Is Heavenly Father's Son."
(1) Review activity (noted in the box above). (2) Color and cut out cradle, baby Jesus, and "x" stand. (3) Fold "x" stand and glue "x" part of the stand facedown in center of cradle. (4) Glue baby Jesus on top of stand.

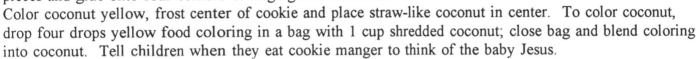

THOUGHT TREAT: Graham Cracker Manger with Coconut Straw. You'll need two graham crackers for each child. Break one cracker apart into four pieces. Frost four pieces and glue onto four corners of large graham cracker. Color coconut yellow, frost center of cookie and place straw-like coconut in center. To color coconut, drop four drops yellow food coloring in a bag with 1 cup shredded coconut; close bag and blend coloring into coconut. Tell children when they eat cookie manger to think of the baby Jesus.

Lesson #6*	LOVE: Heavenly Father and Jesus Love Me *(hearts on-a-string)*

YOU'LL NEED: Copy of hearts (page 9) on cardstock paper for each child, scissors, crayons, and ribbon, yarn, or string

ACTIVITY: Create hearts-on-a-string to remind children that Heavenly Father loves them.

See song activity (page 15) in Primary 1 manual.*

(1) Sing "My Heavenly Father Loves Me," page 228 in the *Children's Songbook** using the following hearts-on-a-string. (2) Color and cut out hearts.
(3) Punch a hole at the top and bottom of each heart.
(4) String ribbon, yarn, or string through heart. Tie together. (5) Allow children to look at images as you sing the song. (6) Place heart necklace around child's neck. (7) Point the child's chest and say, "Your heart is in here."

THOUGHT TREAT: Heart-Shaped Cookies or Candies.
Tell children that Heavenly Father and his son Jesus love us. They gave us this beautiful world so we can be happy. Let's tell them how much we love them when we pray. Let's thank Heavenly Father for: (naming pictures on the hearts): Birds, sky, rain, wind, rose, lilac tree, eyes, ears, body, and butterfly.

Jesus Is Heavenly Father's Son.

PATTERN: *CHILD of God (crown for heavenly prince or princess)*

Lesson #7*   **HOLY GHOST:** The Holy Ghost Helps Me to Be Happy
(Smile and Frown Game with flip sign favor)

YOU'LL NEED: Copy of faces flip sign favor (page 11) on cardstock paper and wooden craft stick for each child, scissors, glue, and crayons
ACTIVITY: Play the Smile and Frown Game to help children vote on actions that make them happy or sad. Have them guess actions that invite the Holy Ghost, and actions that turn the spirit of the Holy Ghost away.

See Enrichment Activity #2 (page 21) in Primary 1 manual*.

(1) Color and cut out a smile and frown. (2) Glue back to back (sliding a wooden craft stick in the center). Help children line up smile and frown so they are not upside down. (3) Talk about the signs: Show smile side and say, "The Holy Ghost helps me to be happy!" Show frown side and say, "I'm sad when I don't choose the right." (4) PLAY THE SMILE AND FROWN GAME: Ask children take turns coming up to the front of the class or do this all together. When teacher says the action children turn sign to smile or frown to vote on the things that invite the Holy Ghost or things that turn it away. Vote on: ♥ Help brother pick up toys (happy). ♥ Push someone (sad). ♥ Come to Primary (happy). ♥ Say thank you (happy). ♥ Poke a friend (sad). ♥ Fold your arms (happy). ♥ Open eyes during prayer (sad). ♥ Yell in the chapel (sad). ♥ Run down the hall (sad). ♥ Share a treat (smile). ♥ Sing (smile). ♥ Help teacher (smile). ♥ Listen to story (smile). ♥ Whisper during the sacrament (smile). ♥ Help mother (smile). ♥ Fight with brother (frown). ♥ Share toys (smile).
THOUGHT TREAT: <u>Smile Sandwich</u>. Break a graham cracker in half, frost in the center to glue together. Then frost a smile on top. Tell children that it's more fun to smile than it is to frown. Sing the "Smiles," page 267 in the *Children's Songbook**.

Lesson #8*   **DAY & NIGHT:** Jesus Created Light for Day and Night
(day and night bracelet)

YOU'LL NEED: Copy of sun circle and stars and moon circle (page 12) on cardstock paper for each child, scissors, paper punch, string or yarn, and crayons
ACTIVITY: Create a day and night bracelet to show children that Jesus created the sun (light for the day) and the moon and stars (light for the night).

See Additional Activity #1 (page 24) in Primary 1 manual*.

(1) Color and cut out circles. (2) Paper punch holes where indicated with a paper punch. (3) Cut a 12" piece of string, thread through holes and tie bracelet to child's wrist. (4) Explain to children that the purpose of the sun is to give us light and keep us warm during the day, and the moon and stars is to give us light at night. OPTION: Sing, "Twinkle, Twinkle, Little Star."
THOUGHT TREAT: <u>Sunshine Cookie</u>. Color sugar cookie dough bright yellow with yellow food coloring (before adding flour). Roll two tablespoons of dough into a ball. Press ball 1/4" flat on an oiled cookie sheet 2" apart. Cut a face in the center and 20 1-inch slits around the sides with a knife. Bake 375° for 7-9 minutes. OPTION: Color dough orange or blue to create star and moon-shaped cookies.

PATTERN: *HOLY GHOST (smile and frown flip sign favor)*

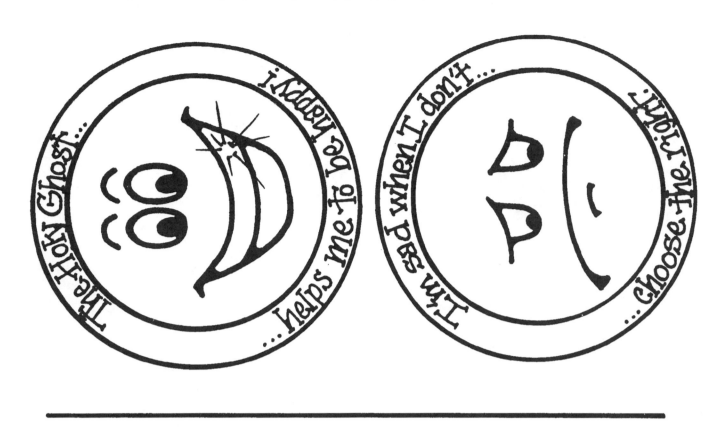

PATTERN: *DAY & NIGHT (bracelet)*

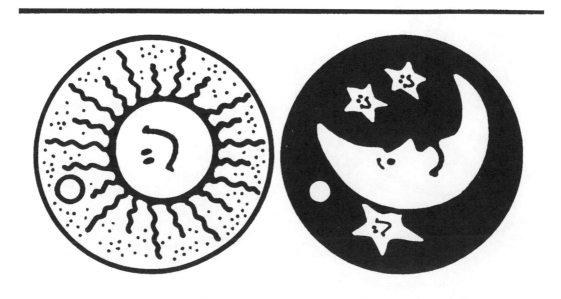

| Lesson #9* | **WATER: I Can Be Baptized in the Water Like Jesus** |
| | *(baptism water wheel)* |

YOU'LL NEED: Copy of sun frame, wheel, and water (pages 14-15) on cardstock paper and a metal brad or button brad for each child, scissors, glue, and crayons

ACTIVITY: Create a baptism water wheel to turn, showing how a child can be baptized in the water (by immersion) like Jesus.

Review "Water Is Important in the Church," (page 26) in Primary 1 manual.*

1. Color and cut out sun frame, wheel, and water.
2. Attach wheel to sun frame with a metal or button brad. To Make a Button Brad: Sew two buttons together on opposite sides (threading thread through the same hole) to attach wheel to sun frame.
3. Glue water to sun frame where indicated.
4. Turn the wheel to show how figures go under the water to be baptized. Tell children that at age 8 they can be baptized in the water like Jesus.

THOUGHT TREAT: Water Cookie. Frost a sugar cookie with blue frosting to look like water. Be sure to give them water to drink and talk about how water is used for many things.

| Lesson #10* | **TREES, PLANTS & FLOWERS: I Am Thankful for Seeds** |
| | *(seed planter)* |

YOU'LL NEED: Copy of cup label (page 16) on lightweight paper, an 8-ounce plastic cup, dirt, and seeds for each child, scissors, tape, and crayons

ACTIVITY: Help children plant seeds in a cup filled with soil to water and watch grow. Talk about the water that keeps plants wet, and the sun that keeps plants warm, helping them to grow.

Review Enrichment Activities #1 (page 29) in the Primary 1 manual.*

1. Color and cut out cup label and tape to cup on sides and bottom.
2. Fill cup 1/2 full, plant seed and fill 3/4 full.
3. Water plant.

THOUGHT TREAT: Seeds or Fruit with Seeds. Share some sunflower or pumpkin seeds and/or fruit with seeds to show and tell.

PATTERN: *WATER (baptism water wheel)*

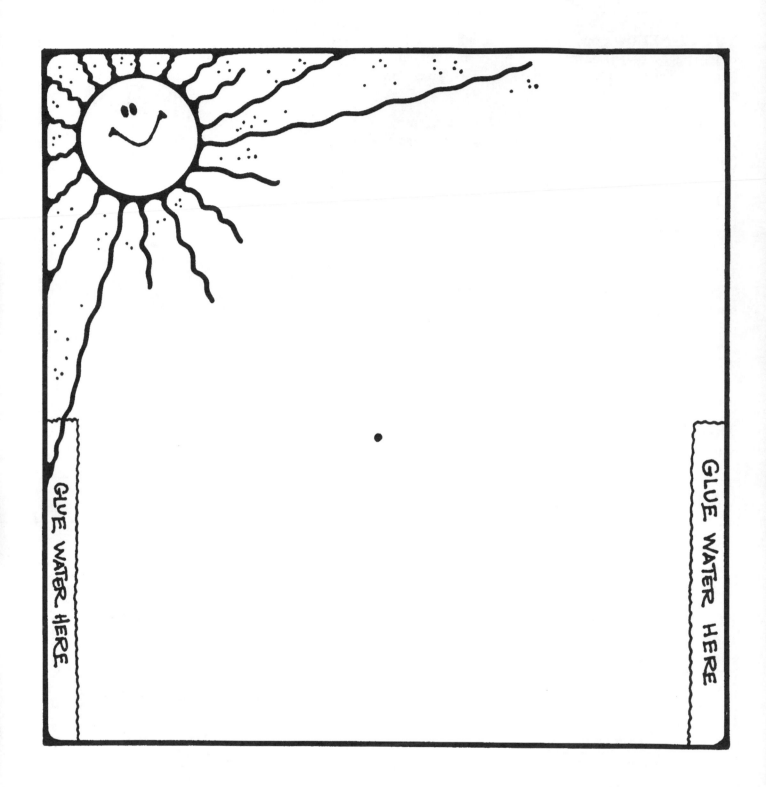

I can be baptized
in the water like Jesus.

Lesson #11*	**FISH & WATER ANIMALS** Were Created by Jesus
	(Jonah and the Whale slide-show)

YOU'LL NEED: Copy of slide-show card (page 18) on cardstock paper for each child, scissors, tape, and crayons

ACTIVITY:
Create slide-show showing Jonah being swallowed by a big fish (Jonah 1-3).

Review Story (pages 31-32) in Primary 1 manual.*

AHEAD OF TIME: Use a razor blade to cut along dashed lines in whale's mouth and water.

1. Color and cut out the whale and pull-through picture strip.
2. Slide (insert) picture strip into slits on the side and in the whale's mouth.
3. Fold back edges of picture strip to prevent pulling all the way out.

THOUGHT TREAT: Idea #1: Squishie Fishies. Create fish-shaped gelatin. Make the firm Jigglers® Jell-o® recipe. Spray pie tins with cooking spray, pour gelatin dessert into pie tins to set up (refrigerate 2-4 hours). Lay firm gelatin onto waxed paper and cut out fish shapes with a knife. Children love the squishie fishie feel as this dessert slithers in their mouth. Idea #2: Fishie Snacks. Candy gummy fish or fish-shaped crackers in a fish bowl or bag.

Lesson #12*	**ANIMALS:** I Am Thankful for Animals
	(favorite animal sticker fun)

YOU'LL NEED: Copy of "I Am Thankful for Animals" sign and animal glue-on stickers (pages 19-20) on lightweight paper, a piece of cardstock paper for each child, scissors, glue, and crayons

ACTIVITY: Create a favorite animal poster.

Review Enrichment Activity #5 (page 37) in Primary 1 manual.*

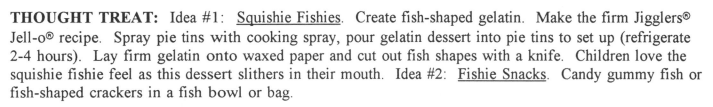

1. Glue the "I Am Thankful for Animals" sign at the top of a sheet of paper.
2. OPTION: Ask children to draw a picture of his or her favorite animals on the paper.
3. Color and cut out the child's favorite animals from the sticker page.
4. Glue animals to poster.
5. Ask each child to tell the other children about his or her favorite animals while holding up poster.

THOUGHT TREAT: Animal Cookies or Crackers.

*Primary 1 manual is published by The Church of Jesus Christ of Latter-day Saints, Salt Lake City, Utah.

17

PULL

Lesson #13*	BIRDS, INSECTS, & CREEPING THINGS I'm Thankful For
	(caterpillar/cocoon/butterfly pull-up and finger puppet)

YOU'LL NEED: Copy of cocoon pocket, caterpillar, and butterflies (page 22) on cardstock paper for each child, scissors, string, glue, and crayons. See #5.
ACTIVITY: Create a visual to show caterpillar going into cocoon and butterfly coming out to show the caterpillar becoming a butterfly.

Review Enrichment Activity #2 (page 40) in Primary 1 manual.

AHEAD OF TIME: Cut slits in butterfly finger puppet and top and bottom pockets of cocoon. (1) Color and cut out cocoon, caterpillar, and butterflies. Color cocoon the same colors as butterfly. (2) Glue outside edge of cocoon 1/4", gluing back to back. (3) Punch a hole at top and thread a string through hole to hang. (4) Slide caterpillar and butterfly in and out (folding butterfly to fit). (5) Option: Copy and cut out story (below) and glue on back of cocoon. Copy and cut out poem (right) to paper punch and attach to cocoon with a string. (6) Tell story.
Butterfly Story: A butterfly begins as a tiny egg that hatches into a caterpillar. The caterpillar eats and grows. It sheds its skin several times as the caterpillar grows to full size. Then it forms a protective shell called a cocoon. When it breaks, its shell opens out into a butterfly. (7) Place a butterfly on child's finger, sliding finger through slits. Child can wiggle finger and watch butterfly fly.

Sing to tune of *Old McDonald*

"Butterflies just flutter by,
  in the flower patch.
 Caterpillars they once were,
  from cocoons they hatch.
 With a flutter here and a flutter there,
  here they fly, there they fly,
  right in front of my two eyes.
 Butterflies just flutter by,
  in the flower patch."

THOUGHT TREAT: Flower Cookie. Purchase or make flower-shaped cookies. Place a gumdrop in the center of a frosted homemade cookie. Tell children to watch the butterflies as they dance from one flower to the next. Watch for them as they flutter by. Sing the song (poem) above to the tune of Old McDonald.

Lesson #14*	ADAM & EVE and Other Creations
	(Days 1-6 creation wristband)

YOU'LL NEED: Copy of wristband (page 23) on cardstock paper, scissors, metal or button brads, glue or tape or pins, and crayons
ACTIVITY: Create a days 1-6 creation wristband children can turn as they think about the creation of the world.

Review Enrichment Activity #2 (page 44) in Primary 1 manual.

(1) Color and cut out creation wristband and days 1-6 spinner.
(2) Attach days 1-6 spinner on wristband with metal or button brad.
To Make Button Brad: Sew two buttons together on opposite sides (threading thread through the same hole) to attach figure to paper. (3) Glue or tape band to child's wrist and turn wheel as you name the days 1-6 creation. Tell them day 7 is a day of rest.
THOUGHT TREAT: Gingerbread Girl or Boy Cookie. Point to Adam and Eve on wristband, saying, "Adam and Eve were our first parents. They were created in Heavenly Father's image."

PATTERN: *ADAM & EVE & OTHER CREATIONS   (Days 1-6 creation wristband)*

Lesson #15*	**SABBATH DAY:** Sunday Is a Special Day
	(Sunday Fun Box Game)

YOU'LL NEED: Copy of box (page 25) on cardstock paper for each child, scissors, glue, and crayons. **OPTION:** Cotton balls.

ACTIVITY: Create a Sunday fun box children can roll to play a game. Children take turns rolling and showing activity that faces up on block, e.g.: Child shows "pray" by folding arms, bowing head, and closing eyes. Other children can follow the leader to copy the Sabbath day action. Children can smile when they roll Sunday Fun Box.

Review Enrichment Activity #1 (page 47) in Primary 1 manual*.

1. Color and cut out block.
2. Fold and glue edges.
3. OPTION: Stuff box with cotton balls.
4. Fold and tape down lid.

THOUGHT TREAT: Sabbath Day Olives. Place an olive on each child's finger to count days 1-6 work days. Tell the story about the pioneers found in the lesson (#2, page 47).

Lesson #16*	**BODY:** Good Food Makes My Body Strong
	(Daniel Eats Good Food mouth pocket)

YOU'LL NEED: Copy of Daniel mouth pocket and food (pages 26-27) on cardstock paper, and an extra sheet of cardstock paper for each child, scissors, and crayons

ACTIVITY: Create Daniel and good food that children can put in Daniel's mouth. Food items shown (left) are nuts, corn, water, bread, rice, and wheat cakes.

#1 See Enrichment Activity #2 (page 50) in Primary 1 manual*.
#2 See Story (page 49) in Primary 1 manual* as you tell of Daniel who ate the food Heavenly Father wanted him to eat. (Daniel 1).

(1) Color and cut out Daniel and food. (2) Cut a slit in Daniel's mouth. (3) Glue Daniel poster to separate piece of paper, gluing sides and bottom only, leaving room for food to drop into pocket. To retrieve food, simply separate top and reach down in.

THOUGHT TREAT: Healthy Foods. Share a variety of tempting good-for-you foods, e.g.: apples, celery with peanut butter, cheese sticks, dried fruit, pretzels, or bananas.

PATTERN: *SABBATH DAY   (Sunday Fun Box)*

Daniel ate good food for a healthy body.

Lesson #17*	HANDS: My Hands Can Help
	(helping hand mitten)

YOU'LL NEED: Copy of mitten (page 29) on cardstock paper for each child, scissors, glue, and crayons

ACTIVITY: Create a mitten showing ways to lend a helping hand: Brush teeth, dress, play ball, wash face, eat, feed cat, and make music. Children slip mitten over their hand and flip mitten back and forth to show ways they can help. The smile reminds children that helping makes them happy. Ask children to come up one at a time and tell others ways their hands can help.

Review Learning Activity: "How do your hands help?" (pages 52-53) in Primary 1 manual*.

1. Color and cut out mittens.
2. Glue mitten together 1/4" on outside edge, leaving bottom open for child's hand to fit in.

THOUGHT TREAT: Thumbprint or Handprint Cookie. Roll cookie dough into balls and press a child's handprint or thumbprint into cookie dough. Sprinkle hand or thumbprint with colored sugar or decorator candies before baking. As children eat their cookie, remind them that Heavenly Father and Jesus created our hands so we could use them to work, play, and get ready for church.

Lesson #18*	EARS: I Am Thankful I Can Hear
	(listen carefully rattle)

YOU'LL NEED: Copy of rattle (page 30) on colored cardstock paper and a wooden craft stick for each child, glue, tape, and crayons

ACTIVITY: Create a rattle children can shake to hear what's inside, and to remind them to thank Heavenly Father for ears that hear.

Review Enrichment Activity #3 (page 59) in Primary 1 manual*.

1. Color and cut out rattle.
2. Fold in half.
3. Fold over side and bottom tabs, then glue or tape.
4. Fill 1/3 full with rice, sand, macaroni, popcorn or beans.
5. Fold top tab and glue.
6. Glue and/or tape a wooden craft stick in the bottom center on back.

THOUGHT TREAT: Marshmallow Ears. Give each child two marshmallows and a round sugar cookie. Cut marshmallow in half and stick to cookie to look like ears (using frosting as glue). Decorate the eyes, nose and mouth with frosting in a tube. Child can eat the other marshmallow as they create the face cookie. Talk about the things you can hear with your ears and then eat the cookie. Things you might hear: Mother's voice, Father telling you to say your prayers, your teacher saying, "Be reverent," your dog barking because he needs some food, and the birds chirping.

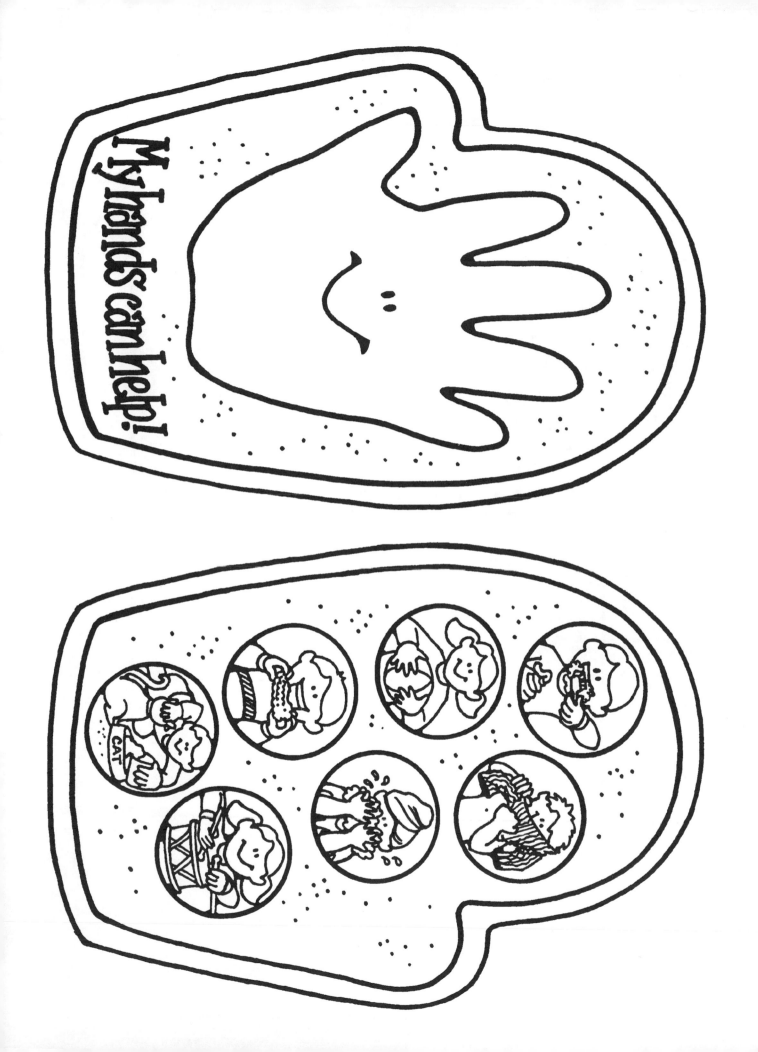

My hands can help!

PATTERN: *EARS (listen carefully flip-flag)*

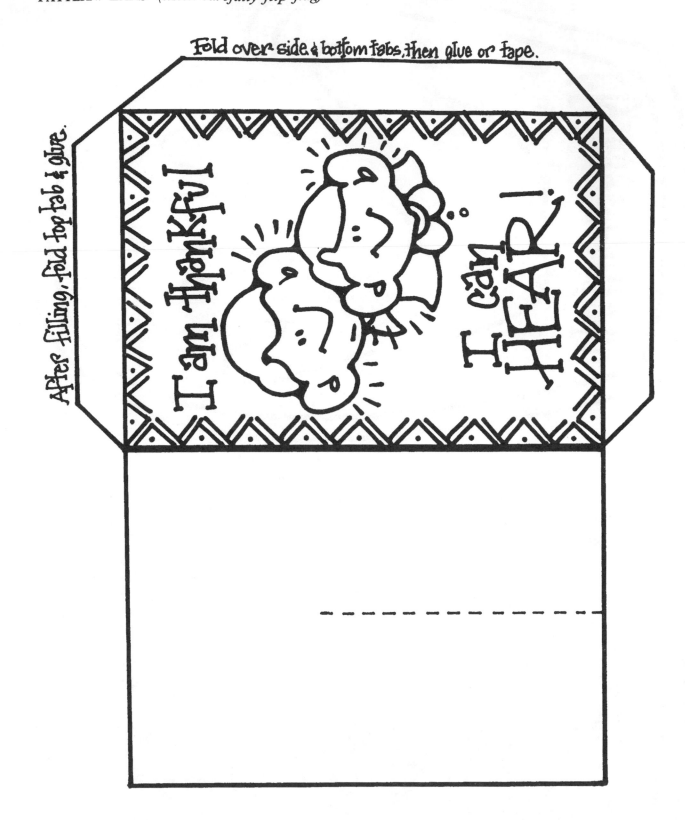

Fold over side & bottom tabs, then glue or tape.

After filling, fold top tab & glue.

I am thankful

I can HEAR!

Lesson #19*	**EYES: I Like to See**
	(glasses with flaps to open and close)

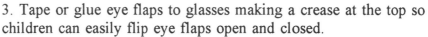

YOU'LL NEED: Copy of glasses and eye flaps (page 32) on cardstock paper for each child, scissors, tape or glue, and crayons

ACTIVITY: Create a pair of glasses for each child with eye flaps that children can flip closed when they want to pretend they are blind. Walk around room with children with eye flaps closed, leading them, and with eye flaps open, asking them to pick up colorful objects.

> *#1 Review the first activity (page 61) in Primary 1 manual*.*
> *#2 Review Additional Activity #3 (page 62) in Primary 1 manual*.*

1. Color and cut out glasses.
2. Tape or glue side pieces on glasses to fit child.
3. Tape or glue eye flaps to glasses making a crease at the top so children can easily flip eye flaps open and closed.

THOUGHT TREAT: Idea #1: Frosted Cupcakes Topped with Gumdrop Eyes. Idea #2: Carrots. As children munch on carrots, tell them that carrots help make their eyes strong so they can see better.

Lesson #20*	**SMELL & TASTE: Heavenly Father Created My Nose and Mouth**
	(cinnamon toast sniff and taste test)

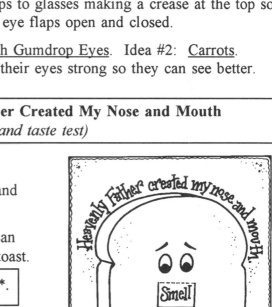

YOU'LL NEED: Copy of cinnamon toast face (page 33) on cardstock paper for each child, glue, sponge, water, cinnamon and sugar, and crayons

ACTIVITY: Create a cinnamon taste and smell test children can enjoy instantly. Then treat them to the real taste of cinnamon toast.

> *Review Additional Activity #1 (page 64) in Primary 1 manual*.*

1. Color toast edge, eyes, nose, and mouth.
2. Cut out "smell" and "taste" signs and tape at the top over nose and mouth on paper toast.
3. Wet a sponge with water and dampen toast part of image.
4. Sprinkle with cinnamon and sugar (3/4 sugar and 1/4 cinnamon).
5. Children can smell and taste the cinnamon and sugar.
6. Children can take this creation home to show, taste-and-smell as cinnamon and sugar doesn't come off.

THOUGHT TREAT: Cinnamon and Sugar Toast. Prepare this ahead. Spread butter on bread and cinnamon and sugar mixture (3/4 sugar and 1/4 cinnamon) on top. Toast on broil 2-3 minutes in the oven (not the microwave). Serve bread cold. Encourage children to sniff and taste. OPTION: Sprinkle multi-colored decorating candies on top of butter, cinnamon and sugar bread before toasting. Children love to pick at the little candies as they eat.

PATTERN: *EYES (glasses with flaps to open and close)*

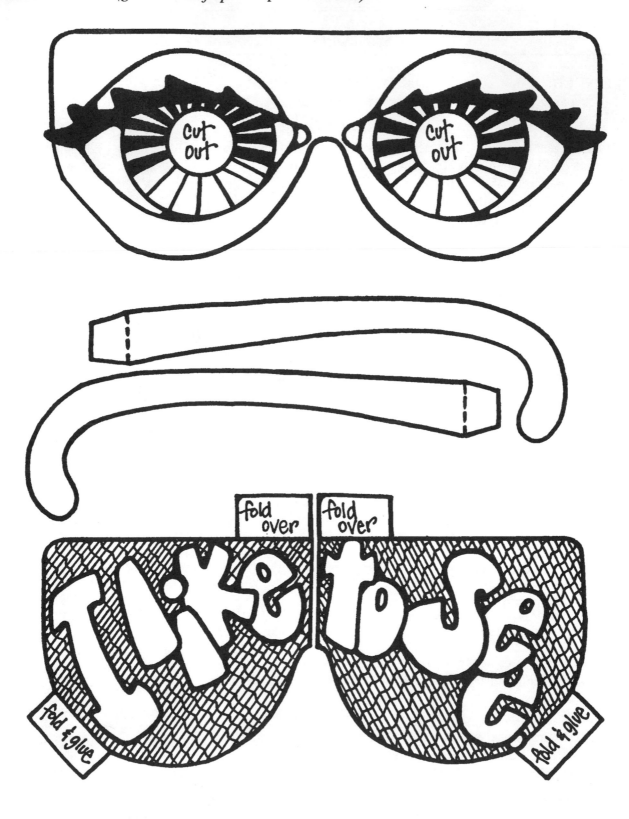

Heavenly Father created my nose and mouth.

fold back & glue on dotted line

Taste

fold & glue

Smell

| Lesson #21* | **FEELINGS: My Feelings Show in My Face**
(feeling faces mobile) |

YOU'LL NEED: Copy of either girl faces for girls or boy faces for (pages 35-36) on cardstock paper for each child, scissors, yarn or string, wooden craft sticks, tape, a hand mirror, and crayons

ACTIVITY: Create a feelings funny face mobile with four faces that show different emotions: happy, sad, angry, and frightened.

> *Review "Our feelings show in our faces" Activity (page 66) in Primary 1 manual*.*

(1) Color and cut out faces. (2) Tape a piece of yarn or string on the back of each face. (3) Tie the other end of the string to two wooden craft sticks. (4) Let each child look into a mirror to practice feeling faces.

THOUGHT TREAT: Clown Funny Face Cookie. Make oatmeal cookie dough. Refrigerate dough covered in plastic wrap at least 1 hour for easier handling. Shape dough into 2" balls. Insert a wooden craft stick into each ball (optional). Place 4 or 5 cookies on each oiled cookie sheet. Flatten ball to 1/4" thickness. Press M&M® or peanut butter candy coated pieces into cookie to shape a face. Bake 350° for 8-12 minutes. Oatmeal Cookie Recipe: 3/4 cup sugar, 3/4 cup brown sugar, and 3/4 cup butter or margarine, 1 1/2 teaspoon vanilla, 2 eggs, 1 1/2 cup plus 2 tablespoons flour, 1 teaspoon baking soda, 1 teaspoon baking powder, 1/2 teaspoon salt, 2 cups rolled oats.

| Lesson #22* | **THINGS: I Can Do Many Things**
(string of I "Can" Do's) |

YOU'LL NEED: Copy of "I Can" cans and glue-on stickers (page 37) on cardstock paper for each child, glue, string, and crayons

ACTIVITY: Create a string of cans with stickers on the back to show the things children

> *Review Enrichment Activity #4 (page 73) in Primary 1 manual*.*

"can" do using the senses Heavenly Father gave them. This is a review of lessons #18-20 in the manual*. Children can take this string of things they can do home to show-and-tell.
1. Color and cut out cans and matching glue-on stickers.
2. Lay a 20" piece of string on the back center of each can. At the same time, glue the matching sticker over the back of the can (over the string). Matching Stickers: Flower (I Can Smell), Apple (I Can Taste), Airplane (I Can See), and Bird (I Can Hear).
3. Talk about the sense of touch (not shown on cans).

THOUGHT TREAT: Treats in a Can. Empty several cans to serve snacks to the children in. Tape top edge of cans to protect against cuts. Larger cans are better to place graham crackers, soda crackers, cereal, and/or dried fruit. Copy an extra set of "can" activities to glue on large cans. You could use these cans each week to remind children of what they "can" do.

PATTERN: *FEELINGS (funny face mobile-girl)*

PATTERN: *FEELINGS (funny face mobile-boy)*

Lesson #23*

FAMILY: Birds of a Feather Stick Together
(bird nest family fun)

YOU'LL NEED: Copy of bird family (page 39) on cardstock paper for each child, scissors, glue, and crayons

ACTIVITY: Create a nest into which children can slip eggs and tiny birds in and out to pretend they are part of a family. Talk about the closeness of a family, how birds really stick together to help one another, how mother bird feeds her young, etc.

See Additional Activity #1 (page 76) in Primary 1 manual*.

AHEAD OF TIME: Cut slits in bird nest with razor blade.
1. Color and cut out nest, eggs, and birds.
2. Slide eggs and birds into slit in nest, or glue into place.

THOUGHT TREAT: Jelly Bean Eggs or Gummy Worms.

Lesson #24*

BROTHERS & SISTERS: We Can Help Each Other
(Baby Moses in the Bulrushes)

YOU'LL NEED: Copy of Baby Moses in Bulrushes (page 40) on cardstock paper, an extra sheet of cardstock paper for each child, glue, and crayons

ACTIVITY: Create a Baby Moses in the Bulrushes scene to describe how a sister helped her brother (Exodus 1:22-2:10).

See Story: Moses in the Bulrushes (page 2, 79) in Primary 1 manual*.

AHEAD OF TIME: Cut slit in basket with razor blade (to enclose baby).
(1) Color and cut out patterns. (2) Slide baby into slit in basket. (3) Move figures around to tell story. Tell how Miriam, the baby's sister, watched over her baby brother until he was safe. Then tell how the Pharaoh's daughter saved Moses from danger (Exodus 2:1-10). (4) Before children go home, glue the bulrushes, Miriam, the baby basket, and the Pharaoh's daughter to the extra sheet of cardstock paper.

THOUGHT TREAT: Baby in a Blanket. Make a hot dog baked inside bread stick dough (shown left). Purchase 8-count ready-made bread stick dough, and eight hot dogs. (1) Cut hot dog in half. (2) Cut 6-inch strips of bread dough in half. (3) Place round edge of hot dog at the top of dough strip. Wrap around the middle and cover bottom. (4) Bake at 350° for 20-25 minutes or until golden brown. (5) Makes 16.

*Primary 1 manual is published by The Church of Jesus Christ of Latter-day Saints, Salt Lake City, Utah.

Families Are Forever!

Lesson #25*	**FAMILY:** I Love My Whole Family
	(Show-and-Tell Family Ties)

YOU'LL NEED: Copy of family cards (page 42) on cardstock paper for each child, scissors, yarn, and crayons

ACTIVITY: Create a string of family members on cards children can tie together with yarn. Tell children that it is important to love their whole family, pray for them, spend time with them, and tell them they love them.

> Review *Enrichment Activity #3 (page 82) in Primary 1 manual**.

1. Color and cut out family members.
2. Punch a hole at the left and right of each card.
3. String yarn through each on the back side.

THOUGHT TREAT: Rope Licorice Tied in Knots.
Tie two pieces of licorice together with a knot. Tell children that this knot in the licorice helps keep the pieces together. Telling your family that you love them is one way to strengthen family ties and "tie" families more securely together.

Lesson #26*	**FAMILIES** Can Be Together Forever
	(temple prep slide-show)

YOU'LL NEED: Copy of temple prep slide show (page 43) on cardstock paper for each child, and crayons

ACTIVITY: Create a temple with pull-through picture strip to show ways we can prepare to go to the temple: pray, obey parents, love others, go to church, pay tithing, and eat good foods.

> Review "I can prepare to go to the temple," *(page 86) in Primary 1 manual**.

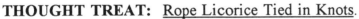

AHEAD OF TIME: Use a razor blade to cut slits in temple on sides of door.
1. Color and cut out the temple and pull-through picture strip.
2. Slide (insert) picture strip into slits on sides of door.
3. Fold back edges of picture strip to prevent pulling all the way out.

THOUGHT TREAT: Temple Mints, or Chocolate Money Coins (to represent tithing).

PATTERN: *FAMILY   (Show-and-Tell Family Ties)*

PATTERN: *FAMILIES (temple prep slide-show)*

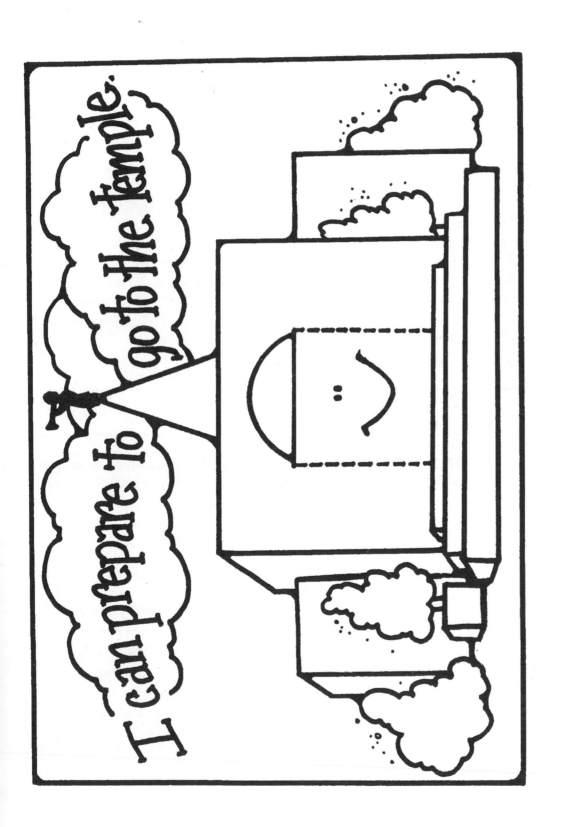

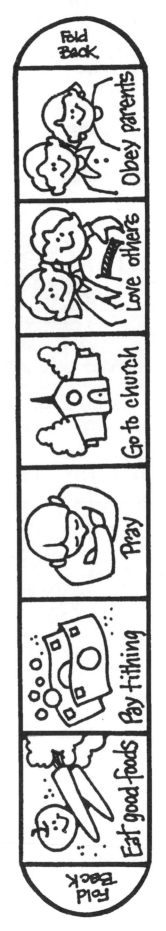

Lesson #27*	**PRAYER with My Family** *(Heart to Heart Family Prayer Chart)*

YOU'LL NEED: Copy of family prayer chart and hearts (pages 45-46) on cardstock paper for each child, scissors, tape, paper punch, string, and crayons

ACTIVITY: Create a chart children can take home to place family names on the hearts. From Monday to Sunday they can place hearts in the day's pocket to show who is giving the family prayer. Talk about the happy feelings we have when we pray together.

Review Enrichment Activity #3 (page 91) in Primary 1 manual.*

AHEAD OF TIME: Use a razor blade to cut slits in day pockets (on chart). To make chart: (1) Color chart, coloring the days in light/pastel watercolor markers. (2) Count the number of people in their family and cut out and paper punch a heart for each family member. Write the child's name on one of the hearts. (3) Punch a hole to the left of chart. Before punching a hole, put a piece of tape behind the designated location to prevent tearing once the strings are attached. (4) Tie a string to each heart (one for each member of the child's family). Tie strings to chart. (5) Show children how to place their heart in their assigned day pocket. (6) Show children how to have a family prayer.

THOUGHT TREAT: Heart Shaped Cookies or Candies.

Lesson #28*	**OBEDIENCE: I Will Obey** *(Fishes and Wishes to Obey)*

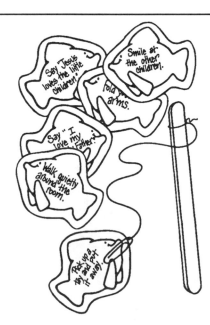

YOU'LL NEED: Copy of fish (page 47) on cardstock paper and a wooden craft stick for each child, ruler, string, paper clips, and light/pastel markers

ACTIVITY: Help children fish to find fun ways to obey. Talk about actions as they throw a string (with a paper clip attached) over a chair to find a fish. Tell children that Heavenly Father wishes us to obey. Let's get some fishes to find out the wishes.

Review Enrichment Activity #3 (page 94) in Primary 1 manual.*

AHEAD OF TIME: Create a fishing pole by tying and taping string to the end of a wooden craft stick. Attach a paper clip at the other end of string. (1) Color edge of fish (not over words unless using light/pastel watercolor markers). (2) Cut out fish. (3) Hook a paper clip to the end of the fishing pole. (4) To fish, child can cast his/her pole over a chair. Place fish on paper clip to pull back. (5) Read each fish aloud, and do the obedient action with the children.

THOUGHT TREAT: Fish Crackers or Gummy Fish.

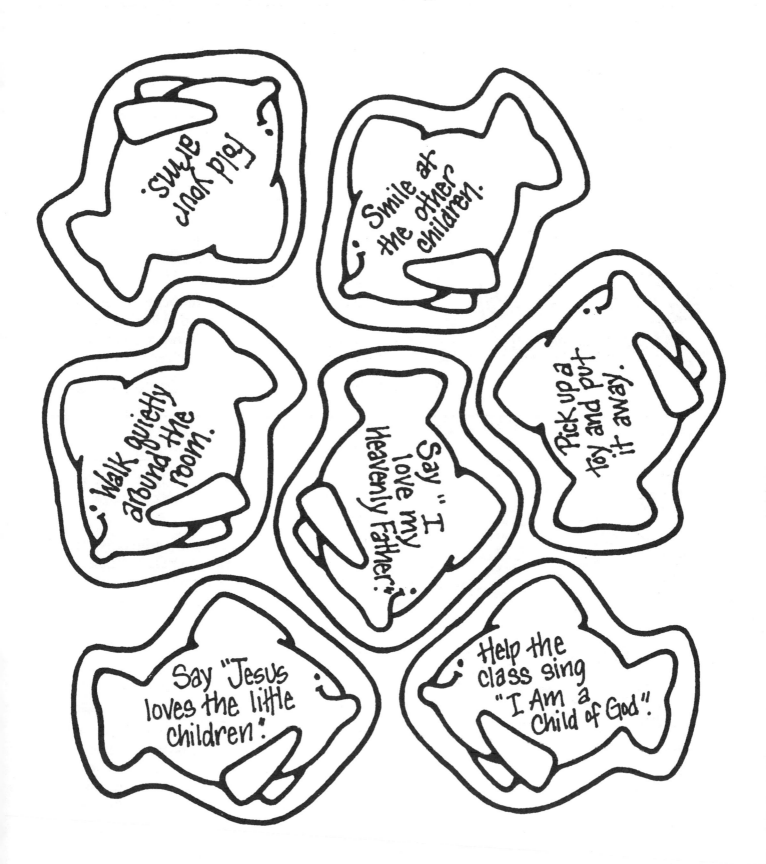

Lesson #29*

SORRY: When I Do Wrong I Say "I'm Sorry"
(steps #1-3 "I'm Sorry" medallion)

YOU'LL NEED: Copy of medallion (page 49) on cardstock paper for each child, scissors, paper punch, yarn, and crayons

ACTIVITY: Create three face circles to show children three repentance steps: #1 Recognize Wrong: "I Did Wrong," #2 Repent: "I Said 'I'm Sorry'," and #3 Happy Feeling: "I Feel Happy Again!"

> *Review Enrichment Activity #2 (page 97) in Primary 1 manual*.*

1. Color and cut out faces.
2. Punch a hole at the top of each face.
3. String yarn through holes, tying a knot between each to separate. Tie at the end and place around child's neck. Make the yarn long enough that child can slide faces along yarn and look at each face to remember the steps of repentance.

THOUGHT TREAT: Frown and Smile Frosted Cookies.

Lesson #30*

FORGIVE: I Can Shine Bright and Forgive Others
(sunbeam badge)

YOU'LL NEED: Copy of Sunbeam badge (page 50) on cardstock paper for each child, yellow or orange yarn, safety pins or paper clips, and crayons

ACTIVITY: Encourage children to beam brightly, as they wear a Sunbeam badge with yarn streamers. Children can look at the picture of Jesus and remember how he forgave others. Sing songs from the *Children's Songbook** as suggested in the lesson: "Jesus Wants Me for a Sunbeam," page 60, or "Jesus Said Love Everyone," page 61.

> *Review Additional Activity #2 (page 100) in Primary 1 manual*.*

MAKE BADGE AHEAD OF TIME (with streamer option): (1) Cut out badge. (2) Cut 4" pieces of yarn and tie streamers on Sunbeam badges (three or four streamers each). (3) Punch three or four holes around edge with a pen or pencil and thread yarn through holes. (4) Tie knot on back end. (5) Children can color sun yellow or orange. (6) Pin badge on child with a safety pin or paper clip.

THOUGHT TREAT: Crackers with Cheese Sunshine. Serve soda crackers and create a sun image on each with processed cheese in a tube.

PATTERN: *SORRY   (steps #1-3 "I'm sorry" medallion)*

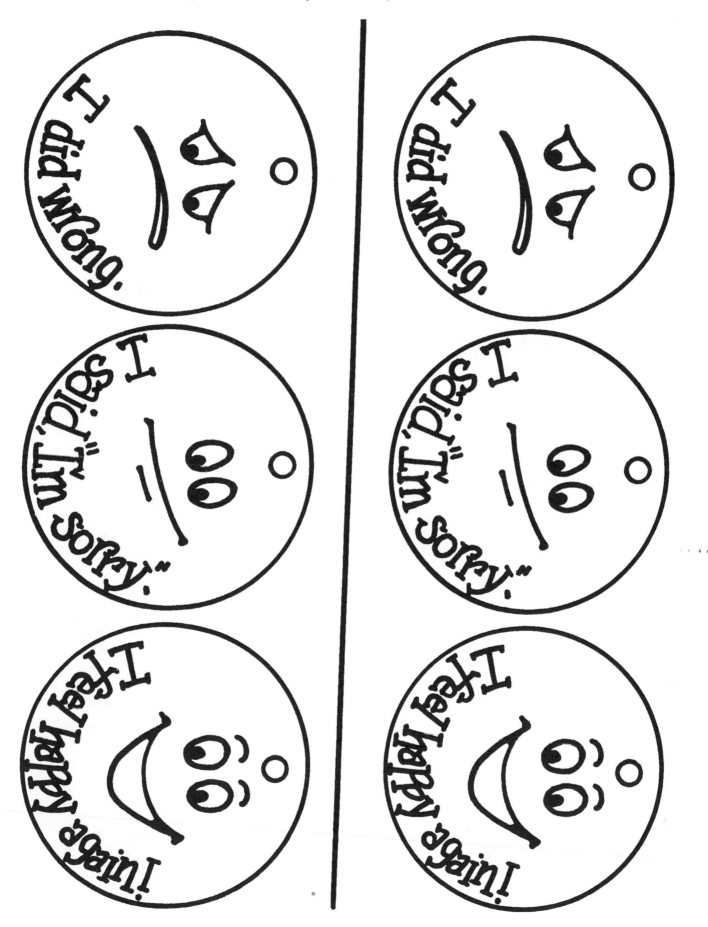

Lesson #31*

HOME: I Am Thankful for My Home
(Home "Tweet" Home charm bracelet)

YOU'LL NEED: Copy of houses (page 52) on cardstock paper for each child, scissors, paper punch, yarn, and crayons

ACTIVITY: Create a Home Sweet Home or Home "Tweet" Home charm bracelet to remind children to be thankful for their home. Use visuals to teach about the various places that birds, fish, animals, and insects live. Show the tent as you talk about Lehi and his people living in the desert (and possibly a toy boat to show how they sailed to the Promised Land), draw a covered wagon as you talk about the pioneers, etc.

1. Color and cut out charms.

> *Review Enrichment Activity #5 (page 103) in Primary 1 manual*.*

2. Punch a hole at the top of each charm.
3. String yarn through holes and tie a knot at ends.
4. Tie around child's wrist. OPTION: Color and cut out two sets of charms to play a match game. With images face down, children take turns turning homes over (two at a time) to make a match.

THOUGHT TREAT: Home-Sweet-Home Cookies. Cut out sugar cookie dough into a house shape.

Lesson #32*

FOOD & CLOTHING I'm Thankful For
(Think and Thank match game)

YOU'LL NEED: Copy one set of match cards (page 53) on cardstock paper for each child, and crayons

ACTIVITY: Create a Think and Thank match game to help children think how we receive food and clothing, and thank Heavenly Father. Talk about the clothing created from the sheep's wool. Talk about milk that comes from the cow. Talk about the apples we can pick from a tree.

> *Review Enrichment Activity #1 (page 106) in Primary 1 manual*.*

1. Color and cut out match cards.
2. To play the Think and Thank Match Game, mix up cards and lay them face up on the table. Help children place the matching cards side by side, saying, "Sheep, thank you for the sweater," "Cow, thank you for the milk," and "Tree, thanks for the apples." Heavenly Father, I thank thee for everything.

THOUGHT TREAT: Animal Crackers with Milk, or Apples.

*Primary 1 manual is published by The Church of Jesus Christ of Latter-day Saints, Salt Lake City, Utah.

51

PATTERN: *HOME   (Home "Tweet" Home charm bracelet)*

sheep

sweater

cow

milk

Tree

Apple

Lesson #33*	**FRIENDS:** I Can "Bee" a Friend (friendship window wheel)

YOU'LL NEED: Copy of window wheel (pages 55-56) on cardstock paper for each child, scissors, metal or button brads, and crayons

ACTIVITY: Children can learn to "bee" a friend as they turn this wheel with the bee pointing to the good deeds: Sharing toys or treats, smiling, or saying "Hi!"

Review Enrichment Activity #4 (page 109) in Primary 1 manual.

(1) Color and cut out window wheels. (2) Attach part A on top of part B with a metal or button brad (placed in center). TO MAKE A BUTTON BRAD: Sew two buttons together on opposite sides (threading thread through the same hole) to attach window wheels.

THOUGHT TREAT: Any Treat That Can Be Shared. Candy bar with squares, graham crackers, chips, small pieces of candy, or licorice. Or, pass out honey taffy, telling children that bees create the honey that makes this taffy. Say, "Let's 'Bee' a good friend and share." Take honey taffy out of wrapper and help children pull it apart to share.

Lesson #34*	**LOVE OTHERS:** I Can Share and Care *(Good Samaritan Show-and-Tell)*

I can love others

YOU'LL NEED: Copy of Good Samaritan Story, picture, and moveable arm (page 57) on cardstock paper for each child, glue, metal or button brads, and crayons

ACTIVITY: Encourage children to learn, then show-and-tell the Good Samaritan story as they move the hand holding the cup up and down to give the man a drink. Tell them Heavenly Father wants us to show love to others.

Review Story (page 112) (page 106) in Primary 1 manual.

(1) Color and cut out Samaritan Story, picture, and moveable arm. (2) Attach movable arm on picture with a metal or button brad. BUTTON BRAD: Sew two buttons together on opposite sides (threading thread through the same hole) to attach arm. (3) Glue story on the back of picture. (4) Review story with children moving arm up and down to give the man a drink.

THOUGHT TREAT: Water and Samaritan Snacks. Share with children bread and fruit. Tell them this is like the food the Good Samaritan shared with the person in need. He showed his love for others. Talk about what children can do to be Good Samaritans, e.g., share their toys and food, smile, and be nice.

  *Primary 1 manual is published by The Church of Jesus Christ of Latter-day Saints, Salt Lake City, Utah.

PATTERN: *FRIENDS   ("Bee" a Friend window wheel—Part A)*

Cut out

"I buzzed on over to a friend. I buzzed on over to bee."

PATTERN: *FRIENDS ("Bee" a Friend window wheel—Part B)*

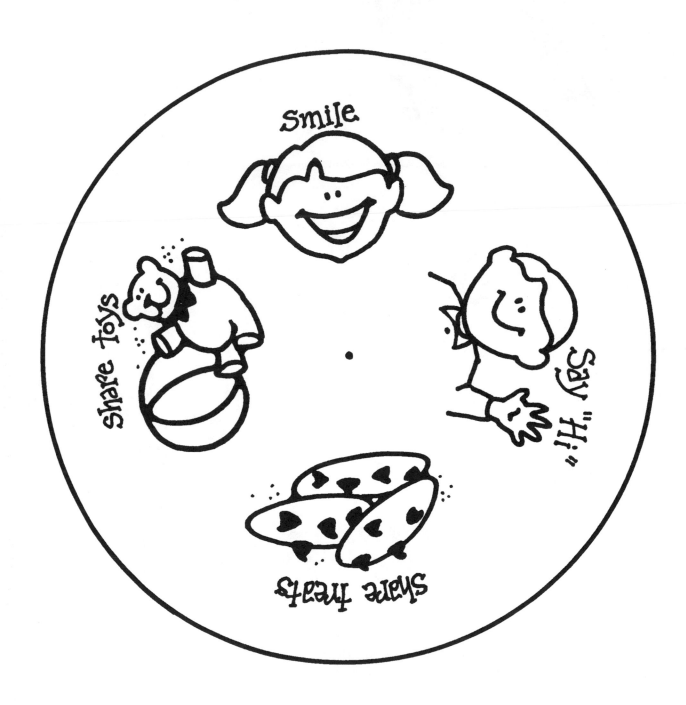

GOOD SAMARITAN STORY - Luke 10:33-34
Jesus told a man how to get to heaven as he told a story.
A man was lying on the road, hurt.
A man saw him and did not stop to help.
A second man saw him and did not stop to help.
Then a Samaritan man stopped to help this poor man.
He gave him water to drink. He put clothes on the man.
He took him to an inn. He gave him money.
Jesus wants us to be kind to others and help.

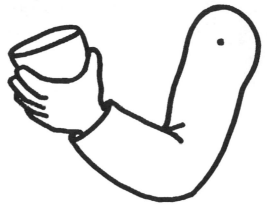

Lesson #35*	**ANIMALS:** I Can Be Kind to Animals
	(Adam Names the Animals slide show)

YOU'LL NEED: Copy of Adam frame and animal pull-through picture strip (page 59) on cardstock paper for each child, scissors, razor blade (to use prior to activity), glue, and crayons

ACTIVITY: Have children help Adam give the animals a name. Create a pull-through picture frame that children can slide animal pictures through as they name each animal.

Review Attention Activity "Adam gave each of the animals a name" (page 115) in Primary 1 manual.*

AHEAD OF TIME: Cut dash lines on left and right side of window in frame with a razor blade).
1. Color and cut out the Adam and Eve frame and animal pull-through picture strip.
2. Slide (insert) picture strip into slits on sides of window frame.
3. Fold back edges of picture to prevent pulling all the way out.

THOUGHT TREAT: Animal Cookies, Fish Crackers, Gummy Worms or Gummy Fish Candies.

Lesson #36*	**EXAMPLE:** I Want to Be Like Jesus
	(picture of me and Jesus)

YOU'LL NEED: Copy of picture frame and children (page 60) on cardstock paper for each child, glue, yarn/string, and crayons

ACTIVITY: Create a picture of Jesus as a child to show children that Jesus once was a little child. Talk about ways children can be like Jesus (ideas below). Sing "Jesus Once Was a Little Child," page 55 in the *Children's Songbook*.

Review lesson ideas "Heavenly Father sent Jesus Christ to earth to be an example for us," (page 119) in Primary 1 manual.*

(1) Color and cut out Jesus picture and girl or boy picture. (2) Glue girl's or boy's picture next to Jesus. (3) Punch holes in frame at the top left and right, and tie yarn or string so child can hang the picture. Tape to the wall until class is over.

THOUGHT TREAT: Footprint Graham Crackers. Frost a footprint on top of graham crackers. Tell children that Jesus loves us and he wants us to follow him, to live as he did.
1. He wants us to be kind (have children take a step forward).
2. He wants us to share our toys (take another step).
3. He wants us to help pick up our toys (take another step).
4. He wants us to be kind (take another step).

*Primary 1 manual and *Children's Songbook* are published by The Church of Jesus Christ of Latter-day Saints, Salt Lake City, Utah.

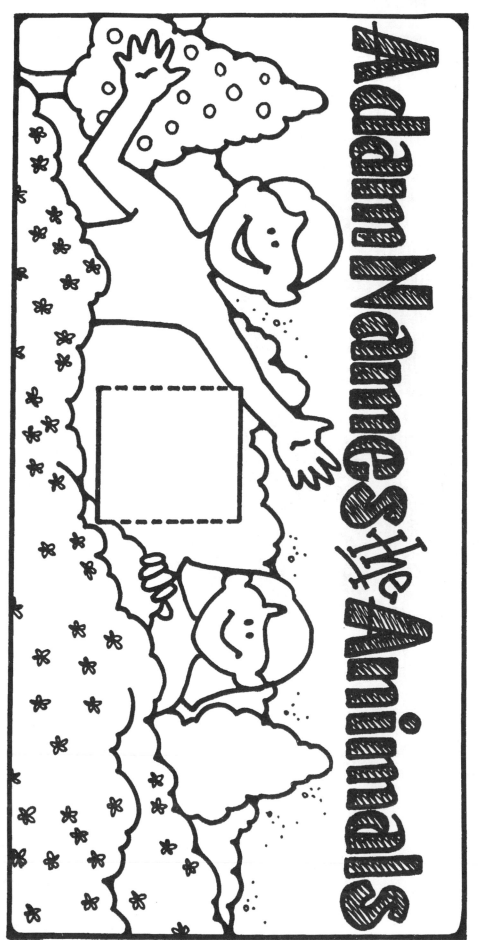

PATTERN: *EXAMPLE   (picture of me and Jesus)*

Jesus once was a little child.

I can be like Jesus.   (see John 13:15)

Lesson #37*	**HONESTY: I Can Be Honest** *(stripling warrior headband)*

YOU'LL NEED: Copy of stripling warrior headband (page 62) on cardstock paper for each child, scissors, glue, and crayons

ACTIVITY: Create an I Can Be Honest stripling warrior headband for each child to remind them to be honest like the stripling warriors. Tell the story found in Alma 53:16-22 and 56:45-57, especially Alma 53:20-21. These men were protected in battle because they were honest. They had faith and courage to do what is right. Children can wear headbands and march around the room pretending to be righteous warriors, proud and happy that they are honest.

Review stripling warrior story and activity (page 123) in Primary 1 manual.*

1. Color and cut out headband.
2. Glue warriors on headband left and right where indicated.
3. Fit headband to child's forehead and tape together.

THOUGHT TREAT: Chocolate Chip or Oatmeal Raisin Cookies. Place cookies inside a cookie jar and have children say, "May I have a cookie from the cookie jar?" Or, "May I have a cookie please?" Talk about the stripling warriors. They loved their mothers and were honest. We too can be honest and ask for things, like cookies from the cookie jar, rather than just taking them.

Lesson #38*	**REVERENCE: I Can Be Reverent at Home and Church** *(Reverence Raccoon story book)*

YOU'LL NEED: Copy of storybook (page 63) on colored lightweight paper for each child, scissors, stapler, and crayons

ACTIVITY: Create a storybook children can learn ways to be reverent and happy at home and church.

See "We can be reverent in church," and "We can be reverent at home," (pages 125, 127) in Primary 1 manual.*

1. Color and cut out reverence story pages.
2. Help children act out reverence actions in story.
3. Staple pages 1-6 together.

THOUGHT TREAT: Marshmallow Raccoon Eyes.
Line a cookie sheet with waxed paper. Place two large marshmallows for each child on tray. Melt marshmallows until light brown. Remove from oven and place a small gumdrop or round candy piece in the center for the eye. Tell children that these look like the eyes of a reverent raccoon. He can see each one of you being reverent.

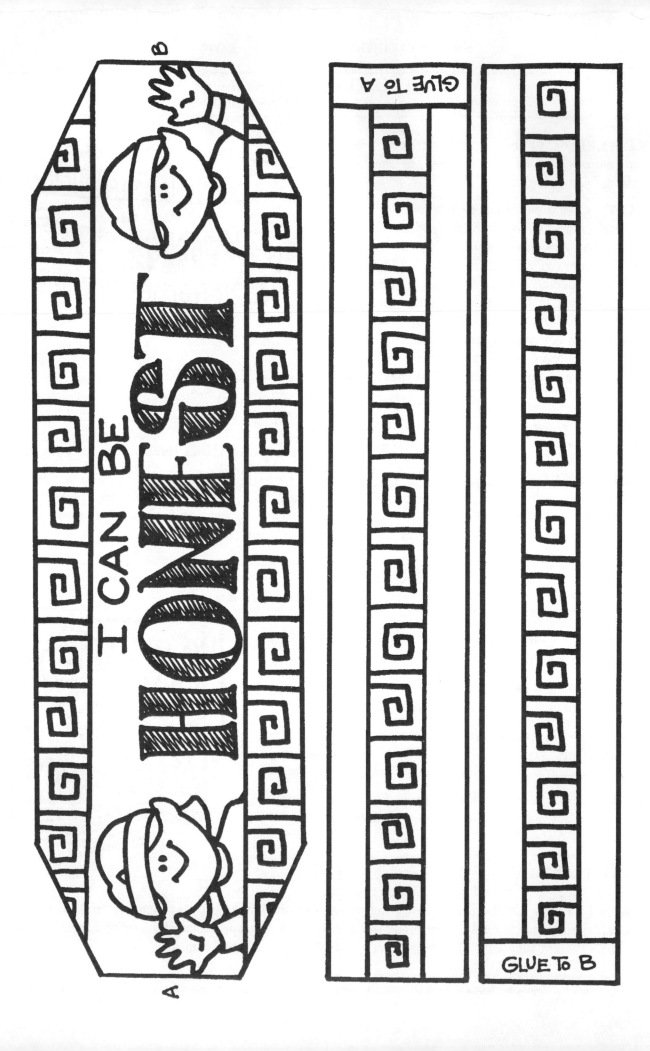

I CAN BE HONEST

GLUE TO A

GLUE TO B

PATTERN: *REVERENCE   (Reverence Raccoon story book)*

Reverence Raccoon was quiet when his family prayed.

He listened at family home evening.

Reverence Raccoon walked quietly at church.

He raised his hand before he talked.

Reverence Raccoon folded his arms during the sacrament.

*Lesson #39**	**MUSIC: Music Makes Me Happy** *(Band Concert instruments)*

YOU'LL NEED: Copy tambourine and shaker labels (page 65) on cardstock paper, two paper cups, two paper plates, and a 11" x 12" zip-close plastic bag for each child, scissors, glue, tape, yarn, rice, popcorn, or beans, paper punch, and crayons

ACTIVITY: Create two instruments children can play to create a musical band concert.
1. Color and cut out labels.
2. Create tambourine and shaker.

Review Enrichment Activity #3 (page 130) in Primary 1 manual.*

3. Shake tambourine with one hand and strike with the other and shake shaker. Shake to the music to create a band concert.
TO CREATE TAMBOURINE: Glue a "Happy Song" label on a paper plate. Place a handful of rice, popcorn, or beans in a zip-close plastic bag, close bag and place bag in the bottom plate. Place a plate on top, punch holes in plate and thread yarn through to sew plate together. Tie.
OPTION: Tie on a few yarn streamers.

TO CREATE SHAKER: Place Music Makes Me Happy smile label on one or two cups. Place a handful of rice, popcorn, or beans in the bottom of one cup. Tape a second cup to the first so that no rice can fall out.

Sing "Happy Song" (page 129) in Primary 1 manual. Pictures on tambourine match.*

THOUGHT TREAT: <u>Sunbeam Gelatin</u>. Create the lemon-flavored Jell-o® Jigglers® recipe. Spray a shallow pan with cooking spray before adding gelatin dessert. Refrigerate 3 hours to set. Turn firm gelatin onto waxed paper and cut out circles to look like suns. Sing "Jesus Wants Me for a Sunbeam," page 60 in the *Children's Songbook*.*

*Lesson #40**	**SACRAMENT: Jesus Loves Me** *(Sacrament Pocket Portrait)*

YOU'LL NEED: Copy picture of Jesus (page 66) on cardstock paper for each child, and crayons

ACTIVITY: Help children carefully color picture of Jesus that they can carry to sacrament meeting to place in their pocket or

Review Additional Activity #1 (page 134) in Primary 1 manual.*

purse. The portrait will remind them to think about Jesus. OPTION: Color ahead and laminate. When coloring use light/bright pastel markers so image show through.

THOUGHT TREAT: <u>Sacrament Smile Cookie</u>. Frost a round sugar cookie with a smile. Tell children that the sacrament helps us to feel happy as we think about Jesus.

PATTERN: *MUSIC (Band Concert paper shaker and tambourine)*

PATTERN: *SACRAMENT (Sacrament Pocket Portrait)*

Lesson #41*	**SCRIPTURES** Contain True Stories *(Book of Mormon Scripture Show-and-Tell)*

YOU'LL NEED: Copy of the six picture stories (pages 68-70) for each child, scissors, glue, zip-close plastic sandwich bags, and crayons

ACTIVITY: Help children learn the true stories of six Book of Mormon heros: Nephi, Abinadi, Alma, Ammon, Captain Moroni, and the 3 Nephites. Children can share stories with their family.

1. Color and cut out picture stories.

Review Enrichment Activity #3 (page 137) in Primary 1 manual.

2. Fold and glue stories on the back of matching picture.

3. Enclose picture stories in a plastic zip-close bag.

THOUGHT TREAT: <u>Scripture Cookie.</u> Roll sugar cookie dough out and cut into open book shapes. Bake and frost cookies. With frosting create a heart on the left and smile on the right. Tell children that the scriptures tell us that Heavenly Father and Jesus love us and this makes us happy. OPTION: Press a piece of red licorice down the center to create a ribbon bookmark.

Lesson #42*	**CHURCH:** I Can Do Many Things at Church *(church charm bracelet)*

YOU'LL NEED: Copy of charms (page 71) on cardstock paper for each child, scissors, yarn or string, and crayons

ACTIVITY: Create a bracelet with four charms to show children the many things they

Review Additional Activity #1 (page 141) in Primary 1 manual.

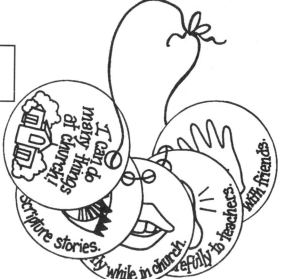

can do at church to show good behavior. Show each picture and talk about the actions. Example: <u>Eye</u> ("read scripture stories"), <u>Hand</u> ("play kindly with friends"), <u>Ear</u> ("listen carefully to teachers"), and <u>Mouth</u> ("speak softly while in church"). To make bracelet: (1) Color and cut out four charms. (2) Punch hole. (3) Thread string through each charm, tying a knot between each to separate. Tie a knot at each end. (4) Tie onto child's wrist.

THOUGHT TREAT: <u>Doll Cookie.</u> Cut out a gingerbread cookie girl and boy. Frost cookie after baking, or paint with cookie paints before baking. To make cookie paints, mix two teaspoons canned milk with food coloring. Spread on cookie dough with paint brush. As children eat cookie, talk about the eyes, hands, ears, and mouth that help us do many things at church.

~Nephi~

I had faith that I could return to Jerusalem to get the brass plates. These were sacred records kept by the prophets.

~Abinadi~

Because of my faith in Jesus Christ, I was willing to die for my testimony (at the hands of King Noah).

Alma

Because of my faith and prayers, an angel appeared to my son and four sons of Mosiah calling them to repentance.

Ammon

I desired to preach the gospel. My faith helped me fight a band of robbers trying to kill King Lamoni's sheep.

~Capt. Moroni~

I used the Title of Liberty flag to encourage my people to have faith in Jesus Christ and fight for liberty.

~3 Nephites~

Because of our faith in Jesus Christ, we were promised we shall never face death.

Lesson #43*	**PROPHET:** I Will Follow the Prophet
	(Noah's Family Obeys puppet show medallion)

We are blessed when we follow the prophet!

YOU'LL NEED: Copy ark and Noah's family (pages 73-74) on cardstock paper for each child, scissors, glue, paper punch, yarn or string, and crayons.

ACTIVITY: Create an ark puppet show. Children can tell how God asked the prophet Noah to build an ark to save his family from the flood. Because his family listened to the Prophet Noah and obeyed, they were saved.

> Review "We are blessed when we follow the prophet," Activity (page 143) in Primary 1 manual*.

(1) Color and cut out ark and family. (2) Fanfold ark. (3) Glue ark together on the left and right sides 1/4-inch (leaving pocket open). (4) Punch holes in ark and family where indicated. (5) Tie a 10" piece of yarn or string between bottom of the ark and Noah's family. Tie a 25" piece of yarn or string on sides of ark to hang puppet show as a medallion around the child's neck. (6) Child places family in ark pocket.

   FUN OPTION: Copy and create the 3-D Noah's ark on pages 4-6 in *Primary Partners* book #1 (see preview in back) under subject "ANIMALS."

THOUGHT TREAT: Prophet Pretzels. Give children a pretzel for each prophet they can name: Noah, Moses, Joseph Smith, Samuel, or others.

Lesson #44*	**HELPING:** The Bishop Helps Me at Church
	(Bishop Brag Bag)

Bishop Brag Bag

YOU'LL NEED: Copy of Bishop Brag Bag label and brag pictures (page 75) on cardstock paper and a zip-close sandwich bag for each child and the bishop, scissors, and crayons.
OPTION: Create a Brag Bag children can give to the bishop.

ACTIVITY: Create a Bishop Brag Bag to show children how the bishop helps at church.
1. Color and cut out bag label and brag pictures.
2. Slip inside a zip-close plastic sandwich bag.
3. OPTION: Place treats inside bag.

> Review bishop Activity and Enrichment Activity #2 and 4 (page 146) in Primary 1 manual*.

THOUGHT TREAT: "Bear-y Gurr-ate" Brag Bag Goodies. Place miniature bear cookies or cinnamon or gummy bear candies in Bishop Brag Bag. Mix treats with popcorn as a filler.

PATTERN: *PROPHET   (Noah's Family Obeys puppet show medallion)*

fold

fold

We are blessed when we follow the prophet !

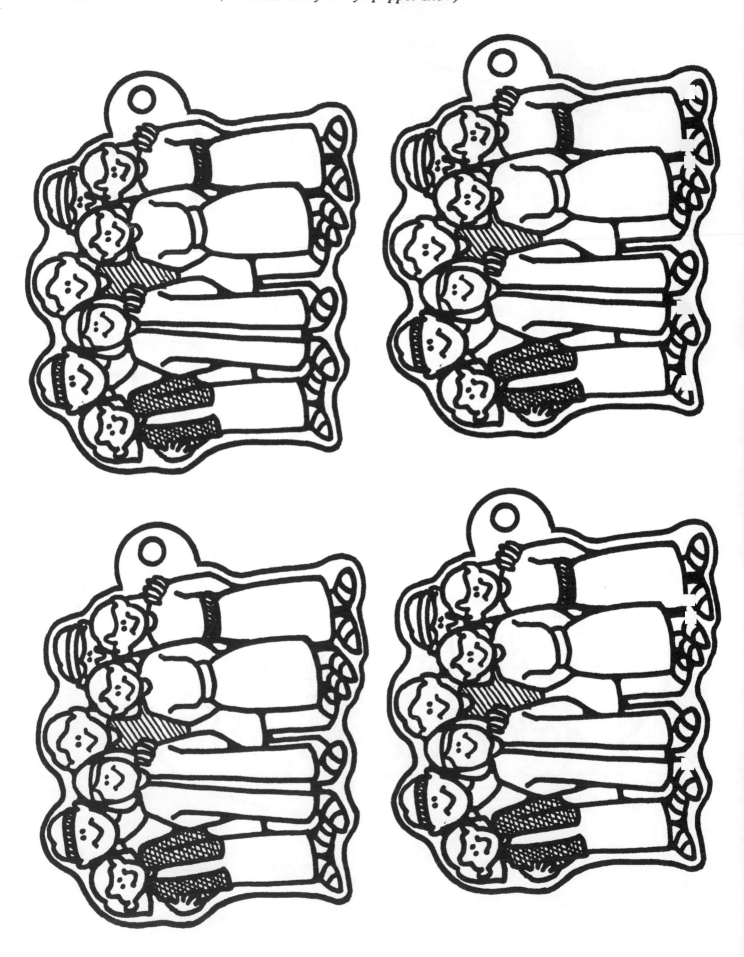

PATTERN: *HELPING (Bishop Brag Bag)*

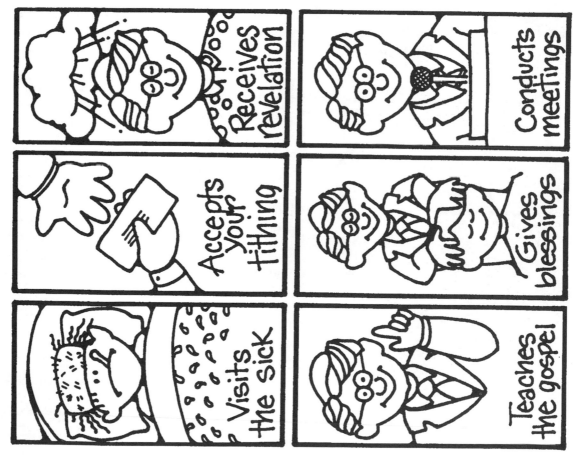

Lesson #45*	EASTER: Jesus Loves Me *(Jesus Loves Me resurrection book)*

YOU'LL NEED: Copy of book pages (pages 77-78) on cardstock paper for each child, glue or stapler, and crayons

ACTIVITY: Create a Jesus Loves Me resurrection book to spotlight the life of Jesus to remind children of the things he did to show his love for us.
1. Color and cut out book pages.
2. Bend tab at top and glue or staple pages together.

> *ADDITIONAL ACTIVITY: Show or create paper dolls with heavenly and earthly home (page 62) in PRIMARY PARTNERS—Volume I Nursery and Age 3 (see "PLAN" in the A-Z CONTENTS in the back of this book).*

THOUGHT TREAT:
New Beginning Basket.
Idea #1: Make an Easter basket using a small round bowl for the

> *Review Additional Activity #2 (page 150) in Primary 1 manual*.*

mold with Rice Krispies® recipe (on box of Kellogg's® cereal). Idea #2: Make a nest using bread dough and bake. Fill basket with candy eggs and tell children that baby birds come from eggs. They are hatched in the springtime. This is the time Jesus died and was resurrected. When we see these eggs, let's remember Jesus, and that he loves us.

Lesson #46*	JESUS WAS BORN: My Gift to Jesus is to Be like Him *(kind deeds advent necklace)*

YOU'LL NEED: Copy of circles (page 79) on cardstock paper and parent note below for each child, scissors, yarn, paper punch, and crayons. OPTION: 12 gold stars for each child placed in a plastic bag.

ACTIVITY: Create an advent necklace children can take home to remind them of kind deeds they can do each day 12 days before Christmas.
(1) Color and cut circles.
(2 Punch holes, and thread yarn through holes and tie.

> *Review Preparation #3 (page 151) and "Our gift to Jesus is to be like him" Activity (page 152) in Primary 1 manual*.*

OPTION: Give each child 12 gold stars in a plastic bag with the parents note (right).

> **PARENTS:** *"Your child is wearing a kind deeds advent necklace. Please place a star on the circle or on the child's forehead for each kind deed your child has done. These kind deeds are your child's gift to Jesus, and the stars represent the star of Bethlehem."*

THOUGHT TREAT: Graham Cracker Gift Box.
Make a gift box by frosting four graham crackers on top of each other (break cracker into fourths). Frost a bow on top. Tell children that Jesus gave us the gift of his life. We can give him a special gift, to live as Jesus lived.

PATTERN: *EASTER   (Jesus Loves Me resurrection book)*

PATTERN: *EASTER (Jesus Loves Me resurrection book)*

Mary H. Ross, Author and
Jennette Guymon—King, Illustrator
are also the creators of

PRIMARY PARTNERS: *Lesson Activities to Make Learning Fun for:*
Nursery and Age 3 (Sunbeams)—Vol. 1
CTR A and CTR B Ages 4-7
Book of Mormon Ages 8-11
Doctrine & Covenants/Church History Ages 8-11
Old Testament Ages 8-11
ACHIEVEMENT DAYS, Girls Ages 8-11

HOME-SPUN FUN FAMILY HOME EVENINGS
Fun For All Ages

MARY H. ROSS, *Author*
Mary Ross is an energetic mother, Primary teacher, and has been an Achievement Days leader. She loves to help children have a good time while they learn. She has studied acting, modeling, and voice. Her varied interests include writing, creating activities and children's parties, and cooking. Mary and her husband, Paul, live with their daughter, Jennifer, in Sandy, Utah

Photos by Scott Hancock, Provo, Utah

JENNETTE GUYMON-KING,
Illustrator
Jennette Guymon-King has studied graphic arts and illustration at Utah Valley State College and the University of Utah. She is currently employed with a commercial construction company. She served a mission to Japan. Jennette enjoys sports, reading, cooking, art, gardening, and freelance illustrating. Jennette and her husband, Clayton, live in Riverton, Utah.

PRIMARY PARTNERS Nursery and Age 3 (Sunbeams)—Vol. 1 PREVIEW

ADAM: Adam and Eve in Heavenly Father's Image (paper doll pleats)

ANIMALS: Thankful For--They Help Me (picture with glue-on stickers)

ANIMALS: Thankful For--Saved From Flood (3-D Noah's ark)

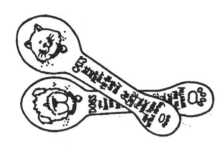

ANIMALS: I Can Be Kind to Animals (cat and dog spoon)

BIRDS & INSECTS: I'm Thankful For (bird watch, bug jar, and "nature walk" binoculars)

BODY: My Body Is Special (body puzzle or hinges doll)

BODY: My Body Looks Like Heavenly Father and Jesus (puzzle)

BROTHERS & SISTERS: I Love You (baby, basket & care items)

CHILD: I Am a Child of God (paper dolls)

CHURCH: Church of Jesus Christ of Latter-day Saints (name badge)

DAY & NIGHT: I Give Thanks (window wheel)

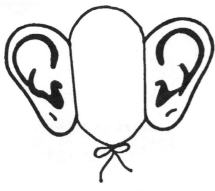

EARS: Ears to Listen and Obey (ear-wings)

EASTER: Jesus Was Resurrected (3-D flower garden)

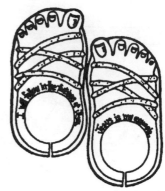

EXAMPLE: Be an Example For Others (follow Jesus sandals)

EYES: My Eyes Help Me to See (giant eyes headband)

FAMILY: I Am Part of a Family (family face block game)

FAMILY: I Love You (family tree with glue-on stickers)

FAMILIES: Together Forever (temple tie and tithing purse)

FEELINGS: My Sunshine Face (smile and frown flip-flag)

FISH & WATER ANIMALS: Fishy Fun (fish, fish bowl, pole)

FOOD & CLOTHING: I'm Thankful For (stand-up card)

FORGIVE: Jesus Wants Us to Forgive Everyone (Joseph/brothers puppets)

FRIENDS: I Can "Bee" a Friend (friendship necklace)

HANDS: I Am Thankful for My Hands (hand-some bracelet)

HELPING: I Can Help at Church (slide show)

HOLY GHOST: The Holy Ghost Is My Helper (gift package)

HOME: I Am Thankful ("Home Sweet Home" job jar and jobs)

HONESTY: I Am Happy when I Am Honest (smile/frown puppet)

JESUS WAS BORN: I Love the Baby Jesus (manger scene)

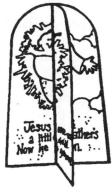

JESUS: Jesus Is Heavenly Father's Son (3-D stand-up card)

LOVE: Heavenly Father and Jesus Love Me (picture and mirror)

LOVE OTHERS: I Can Love Others (spiral kite)

MUSIC Makes Me Smile (music charm bracelet)

OBEDIENCE: I Have "Bean" Obedient (bean bag)

PLAN: Heavenly Father Has a Plan for Me (paper doll with home)

PRAY: To Heavenly Father I Will Pray (Daniel & lions' drama scene)

PRAYER: I Like to Pray with My Family (family prayer fan)

PROPHET: I Know the Prophet Lives (prophet poster fold-out pictures)

REVERENCE Begins With Me (church mouse maze)

SABBATH DAY: Sunday Is My Best Day (creation collar)

SACRAMENT: I Like to Remember Jesus (manners match game)

SCRIPTURES From Heavenly Father and Jesus (scripture specs)

SMELL & TASTE: I Am Thankful For (giant nose and tongue mask) 76, 78

SORRY: I Can Say Hippopotamous and I'm Sorry.

THINGS: I Can Do Many Things (shirt with buttons sewing card)

TREES, PLANTS, & FLOWERS: Creator's Garden (bracelets)

WATER: It's a Wonder (umbrella with raindrop glue-on stickers)

More *PRIMARY PARTNERS*

Each activity is listed alphabetically and cross-referenced to a particular lesson in the Primary manuals. With appealing artwork and fun-to-do games and crafts children will remember the message taught. Use these every week in Primary, of course ... but don't forget family home evening, where the good times get even better.

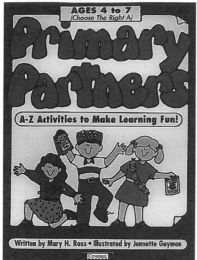

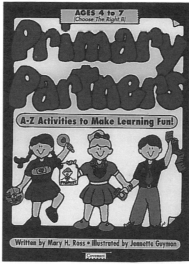

To help children ages 4-7 Choose The Right, enjoy using these 46 ideas/activities from the Primary 2 - CTR A volume to send them home with fun visuals: A pair of resurrection glasses to make the statement, "All eyes can see again!" Or, children can wear a band-aid bandelo to show that "When it is sick that I am feeling, I'll let the priesthood do the healing." These growing spirits can learn about tithing, service, forgiveness, reverence and more.

♥ Heavenly Family Photo
♥ Choices situation slap game
♥ Ammon "script"ure scene
♥ Forgiving Faces
♥ CTR happiness wheel (right)
♥ Prayer rock poem
♥ Dare to Be True wristbands
♥ Gratitude Gopher grab bag
♥ I Love You pop-up card
♥ Scripture scroll
♥ Wise and foolish man flip-flag

As the Primary lesson subjects for ages 8-11 coordinate with the adult scriptures taught, both child and parent can enjoy reading the scriptures together year-after-year. For example, this *Primary Partners* activities match with the Book of Mormon lessons in the Primary 4 manual.

Children this age enjoy challenges to help them develop faith in Jesus Christ, put on the armor of God, keep baptismal covenants, and be a good example, like the heroes found in the Book of Mormon.

Some Testimony Builders Are:
♥ Fight for Right! word choice
♥ 3-D box with Tree of Life Vision
♥ Nephite & Lamanite peace poster
♥ Waters of Mormon word search

Primary 3 - CTR B features 47 more activities to make learning fun:
♥ Annabelle Accountable, the "udderly" responsible cow (left)
♥ Blessings from Baptism picture word poster
♥ Do Unto Others golden ruler
♥ Monday-Sunday prayer elevator
♥ O"bee"dience meter
♥ Sacred Grove moveable scene
♥ Tithing bills match game

These are just a few ideas to teach gospel basics. You'll enjoy the "Chews" the Right gum ball machine into which children can insert a CTR coin and learn seven ways to follow Jesus. Children can learn to fast by placing fruit messages on the fasting tree, e.g., My tummy is empty but my spirit is full. When I go without I won't pout.

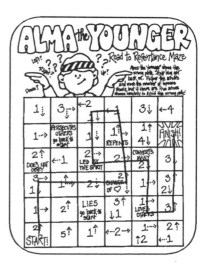

Home-spun Fun FAMILY HOME EVENINGS

Build testimonies with the Articles of Faith 13 Lucky Numbers game.

Tired of those one-size-fits-all family home evening manuals, where the lesson and activities never quite seem to match the ages and stages of your children? Well, your problems are over! In this action-packed, fun-filled volume of fabulous lessons, games, activities, and treats, you'll find something for everyone, no matter what their age!

Whether your family has young children, grade school youngsters, teenagers, or a combination, you'll find age-appropriate games and activities for each of them in virtually every section.

Using the dozens of great lesson and activities in this book, you'll be able to help your children learn and understand basic gospel principles. And you can make each lesson as simple or elaborate as you wish.

You'll find these and more activities to make learning fun:

- ♥ "Bee"atitude cross match
- ♥ Child of God paper dolls
- ♥ Faith is Cool! glasses
- ♥ Faith-ful Saints guessing game
- ♥ Forgiving Faces flip chart
- ♥ Puzzled About Prayer crossword
- ♥ Priesthood Heals band-aid bandelo
- ♥ Sabbath Day Drama or Draw
- ♥ Sacrament manners match game
- ♥ Bear Testimony secret message
- ♥ Tithing origami purse/wallet
- ♥ Word of Wisdom voting ballot
- ♥ Baptism Promises picture/ word poster

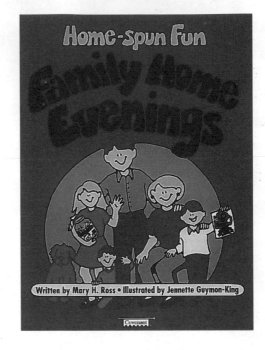

Written by Mary H. Ross • Illustrated by Jennette Guymon-King